MARTIN CLASSICAL LECTURES

MARTIN CLASSICAL LECTURES

These lectures are delivered annually at

OBERLIN COLLEGE

on a foundation established in honor of

CHARLES BEEBE MARTIN

LONDON : GEOFFREY CUMBERLEGE
OXFORD UNIVERSITY PRESS

Classical Influences
In Renaissance Literature

MARTIN CLASSICAL LECTURES
VOLUME XIII

BY

DOUGLAS BUSH

PUBLISHED FOR OBERLIN COLLEGE

BY

HARVARD UNIVERSITY PRESS

CAMBRIDGE : MASSACHUSETTS

1952

THE MARTIN CLASSICAL LECTURES
VOLUME XIII

The Martin Foundation, on which these lectures
are delivered, was established by his many friends
in honor of Charles Beebe Martin, for forty-five
years a teacher of classical literature and classical
art in Oberlin College.

PREFACE

THE PRESENT volume offers two lectures which were delivered at Oberlin under the Martin Lectureship Foundation during the autumn of 1947. Because of circumstances beyond anyone's control, four years have unfortunately elapsed between the delivery and the printing of the lectures. However, since a broad survey of such a subject is relatively unaffected by books and articles that have appeared in the interval, it has seemed best to publish the lectures as they were originally given.

CLASSICAL INFLUENCES
IN RENAISSANCE LITERATURE

I VALUE the honor of being invited to contribute to a distinguished series of classical lectures, and I am glad to have been assigned so congenial a theme. I hope it may be as agreeable to others as it is to me to think for a while about things that are remote from atomic warfare, though they are not remote from enduring realities. And if our broad survey of a familiar field is not studded with new ideas, it may be said that a good many old ideas are worth dwelling upon. Writers and readers in our own time may share some attitudes of Renaissance writers and readers, but we seem to have lost some other elements of a healthy and well-balanced vision, and the most cursory review of a great epoch is salutary.

I

Classical influence on the literature of the Renaissance is a huge subject. It requires a minute survey of antiquity, the Middle Ages, and the Renaissance, the whole web of life, thought, and literature in half a dozen countries during many centuries. One could try to cover the vast territory with the factual and even-handed justice of an encyclopaedia article, but the result would be painfully arid. On the other hand, to stick to two or three major topics, such as the

complex and all-embracing influence of Plato
and Cicero, would be to offer a sketch of the
sun and moon as a picture of the universe. For
instance, if we were to discuss the influence of
Plato, we should need more than two hours to
consider Plato's own thought, Neoplatonism,
the assimilation of Platonic elements into early
Christianity, the development of the tradition
in the Middle Ages, the continuance of Neoplatonism in the Renaissance along with renewed
study of Plato himself, the work of such earnest
Christian Platonists as Marsilio Ficino, the
great translator and expositor; and then the various kinds of Platonic and Neoplatonic influence ranging from the work of Erasmus, More,
and Sir Thomas Elyot to the religion of beauty
in women or the scientific thought of Copernicus and Galileo. So it seems best not to put all
our eggs in one basket, even a Platonic one, but
to scramble them.

It is hardly necessary to say that, while one
has to generalize freely, all generalities are subject to many exceptions and qualifications.
Among many things that must be omitted, apart
from occasional reference, is the great mass of
writing in Latin, both utilitarian and imaginative; the names of Ficino, Erasmus, and More
are sufficient reminders that literature in the international language was of the first importance,
but a large part of it has sunk below the horizon.
Finally, some things will have to be taken for

granted, such as the different and the changing
social, economic, political, and religious condi-
tions in the various countries, the effects of geo-
graphical discovery, and other factors outside
of literature proper. Some modern historians,
by the way, seem inclined to explain the Renaissance in terms of these causes and to minimize
classical influence, but it is difficult for anyone
concerned with literature and thought to follow
them.

The classical revival of the 15th and 16th centuries was a great example of the logical and in-
evitable recurrence of an historical pattern. In
ancient times, when Greek civilization had run
its course, Greece was conquered by the virile
and relatively uncivilized Romans. The Romans
absorbed, in their own way, the culture of
Greece and, under the expanding dominion of
Rome, Graeco-Roman culture spread over most
of Europe, to be in time penetrated, not without
conflicts, by Christianity. Then the empire in
its decay was overrun by the virile and uncivilized barbarians, and once again the conquerors
had to be educated by the conquered, now in a
more or less Christian world. That long process
of re-education was the Renaissance. At first
there were, from Italy to Ireland, only a few
oases of Graeco-Roman-Christian culture, which
flourished because of undisturbed continuity or
quick revival. One conspicuous early phase was
the Carolingian Renaissance. By the 12th and

13th centuries the movement had gained much greater breadth and momentum; it embraced science, philosophy, literature, and art. Thus the rich and many-sided Renaissance of the 15th and 16th centuries, which we think of as *the* Renaissance, was only the brilliant climax of the process of a thousand years. And indeed we should not say "climax," since two important impulses of the Renaissance, sceptical rationalism and experimental science, developed mainly in later centuries and cannot be said to have generally dominated thought and life until the 20th.

All this, to be sure, is commonplace, but in looking at literature we need to keep the large perspective in mind. If we do, we shall not, like some of the early humanists and some nineteenth-century historians, fall into the delusion of seeing the Renaissance as a sudden phenomenon — though the contagion of enthusiasm, the invention of printing, and other causes made the later stages relatively rapid. We shall not, moreover, in thinking of the classical revival in the various European countries, assume that all the cultural clocks are running on the same schedule. And we shall not be surprised by the stubborn vitality, throughout the Renaissance, of medieval books, attitudes, and ideas, or by what often seems to be an incongruous mixture in individual minds; we have the same kind of mixtures in our own age and in ourselves. Per-

haps it should be added that the word "medieval," which I just used, was not a synonym for
"bad" or "muddle-headed." If the classical revival produced rich fruit and not mere wax
flowers, one main reason was the strength of
medieval and Christian traditions and beliefs.

In the history of the various countries — and
in that of individual writers — the classical
Renaissance had three natural stages, discovery,
assimilation, and re-expression. The story of the
discovery or rediscovery, in the 14th and 15th
centuries, of Latin and Greek manuscripts has
been told at large by such scholars as Voigt,
Symonds, Sandys, and Sabbadini, and it is an
often dramatic and exciting story, but it can be
only touched upon here. The early humanists
who hunted so eagerly for manuscripts, and who
brought to light so many neglected and forgot-
ten works of ancient literature, were likely to
heap contempt upon the churchmen and scholastics who had allowed them to gather dust in
cathedral and monastic libraries. Such contempt was doubtless pardonable. But we should
remember some other facts as well: that many
of the chief works of Latin literature, as wholes
or in parts, and Latin translations of some Greek
writings, had been studied throughout the Middle Ages; that a knowledge of Greek had flourished or at least existed at some periods in some
places in various countries of the West; that it
was largely through the labors of generations of

monks that the manuscripts were there to be found; and, finally, we might wonder if a humanist who visited the classical sections of our public and college libraries might not find some dust.

Under the heading of discovery and propagation we may remind ourselves again of the importance of printing. Though much early, and much later, printing could hardly bear comparison with manuscripts, the rapid multiplication of texts by the printing press obviously and immensely hastened the circulation of all kinds of knowledge. A special place in the history of the classical revival has always been given to Aldus Manutius of Venice, the great scholar-printer who issued so many noble editions of Greek and Latin authors. Later in the 16th century there was the French family of scholar-printers, the Estiennes, who themselves wrote important books, dictionaries and other things.

Along with printers must be remembered the countless scholars, from Erasmus and Budé and Vives down to the more or less obscure, who edited the classical authors, who did all the inglorious but essential journey-work of scholarship, who wrote the books that re-created the ancient world as an historical scene, and who adapted the principles and practice of ancient education to the use of modern and Christian peoples. A number of these scholars, among them some whose elegant Latin won them posts in the papal service, had literary zeal unhampered by morals or manners, such as Poggio Bracciolini, hunter of manuscripts, moral essayist, and compiler of a book of off-color anecdotes, whose conscience, late in life, impelled him to marry and, as a prelude, to cast off his mistress, the mother of his fourteen children. Some highly respectable men were pure scholars, devoted to philological and historical learning, such as Budé (who was said to have made the sacrifice of working only three hours on his wedding day), though even he wrote a treatise on education. Still others, like Erasmus and Vives and Melanchthon, were Christian humanists in a full, broad, and active sense. For them classical learning was a means rather than an end. They looked back "to the fountains," pagan and Christian, to find a working ideal for the civilization of the present and future. We shall be coming back to that ideal; indeed we can seldom get far away from it.

Literature includes the literature of knowledge as well as of power, and we must take some account of that heterogeneous mass of writing if we are to appreciate the full effects of the classical revival. There could be no advance in knowledge until men had first caught up with the achievements of antiquity. In the realm of mere knowledge, accordingly, the scholars and teachers who were editing, translating, and propagating the classics were the party of progress; they were leading mankind back to the main road of civilization, from which it had wandered into what they looked upon as the arid desert of scholasticism. Since we cannot survey all the branches of knowledge, we will take two diverse examples, the development of science and the development of historical writing.

We do not now think of the Middle Ages as a long blank period in the history of science. Some names and facts have of course been familiar for centuries, and recent historians have revealed a far greater range of genuine scientific activity than earlier writers suspected. Yet it remains true that most of the great and less great minds were preoccupied with other things than science, and that what we should call a scientific attitude was uncommon. For a representative treasury of early medieval misinformation, there is Bishop Isidore of Seville's encyclopedia, the *Etymologies.* One random item, which is undoubtedly true, will not be found in the *Britannica:* "If an eel is killed in wine, people who drink of it have an aversion for wine." But we might quote more central observations on astronomy and physiology:

> The sun, which is made of fire, develops a whiter heat because of the extreme speed of its circular motion. Its fire, philosophers say, is fed with water, and receives the virtue of light and heat from a contrary element. Hence we see that it is often wet and dewy.

The spleen has its name from being a *supplement* to
the liver, on the opposite side, so that there might be
no vacuum, and this some men think was formed on
account of laughter. For it is by the spleen that we
laugh, by the bile we are angry, by the heart we are
wise, by the liver we love. While these four elements
remain, the creature is whole.[1]

Nine centuries later, in the notable year 1543,
came the revolutionary works of Copernicus on
the astronomical system and Vesalius on the human body. From this time onward the story of
science may be called a story of continuous and
sometimes spectacular progress — though we
may remember that the works of Isidore and his
kind were printed and reprinted throughout the
Renaissance "enlightenment," and that a geo-
centric world, astrological medicine, and similar
doctrines held their ground until well on in the
17th century. If we ask what Copernicus and
Vesalius have to do with the classics, the answer
is that influence was both direct and indirect.
Copernicus, in seeking an explanation of phe-
nomena more economical than Ptolemy's, owed
something to ancient theories of the earth's
movements and to mathematical Neoplatonists
of the Renaissance. In biology and medicine
there were the treatises of Aristotle and Theo-
phrastus, of Hippocrates' followers and Galen,
which helped to establish an attitude and a
method; these works, whatever their errors,
were records of the interrogation of nature, not

uncritical repetitions of traditional and half-occult lore.

As for the indirect influence of the classics, we may approach it by way of Bacon's censure of scholastic logic and the pseudo-sciences as two of the three principal diseases that had hindered the advancement of learning.[2] Scholastic philosophy, originally a great demonstration of faith in human reason and the right of inquiry into the nature of man's world, had come to be the antithesis of the scientific attitude, and Bacon was disposed to condemn both root and branch. The scholastic fallacy, as Bacon saw it, was an unfruitful devotion to logic and metaphysics, to unknowable final causes, along with indifference to observed fact and to the consequent extension of man's power over nature. Although Bacon's scientific aims were different from, in some ways antagonistic to, those of most classical humanists, he and others inherited their hostility to degenerate scholasticism. The general impetus of humanism, the quest of real and useful truth freed from medieval accretions, had a very great influence in stimulating the spirit of critical inquiry and thus in creating an atmosphere favorable to the growth of science.

If as a rule the classical humanists, with such exceptions as Rabelais, took relatively small interest in science itself, and hence came in time to be regarded by the scientific as a party of reaction rather than of progress, one reason was

that the humanists were concerned, not with
man's control over nature, but with the much
harder problem of man's control over himself.
Further, the ethical idealism that the humanists
imbibed from the ancient moralists and the
Christian tradition was not altogether in har-
mony with the behavioristic view of man in-
augurated by such diverse explorers of anatomy
and motivation as Vesalius and Machiavelli;
and Bacon, in his role of practical psychologist,
gave thanks to Machiavelli and others "that
write what men do, and not what they ought to
do." But if Erasmus, for instance, continually
upheld the Christian and classical ideal of what
men ought to do, he also, more than any other
individual, awakened the conscience of Europe
to the folly and wickedness of what men did do;
and Vives, who shared fully in Erasmus' religious, moral, and educational effort, was at the
same time a realistic pioneer in psychology and
sociology.

When we turn to our second example of
classical influence in the field of knowledge, the
understanding and the writing of history, we
find a parallel process. Medieval world-histories and chronicles, apart from a few remark-
able books like Bede's *Ecclesiastical History,*
were likely to be tendentious works in the tradition — though not on the level — of Augustine's
City of God, or uncritical compilations of fact
and legend, or unphilosophical annals of con-

temporary events like the Anglo-Saxon Chron-
icle.   Of the Greek and Roman world in particular, few medieval men approached an historical view.   The "matter of Rome the great"
included the myths and legends of Troy, Thebes,
Alexander, Julius Caesar, and almost anything
else not contained in the matters of France and
of Britain.   One notable example of romantic
historiography is the legend of New Troy,
which was firmly established by Geoffrey of
Monmouth in the 12th century and was not
finally demolished until the early 17th.   Ac-
cording to this legend, Britain, like other nations of western Europe, had an eponymous
Trojan ancestor.   Brutus or Brute, a great-
grandson of Aeneas, having to flee westward,
settled with his followers in Albion and became
the progenitor of a long line of kings. The many
related stories were rehearsed by generations of
chroniclers and celebrated by Elizabethan poets
and dramatists; Shakespeare's contribution was
of course *King Lear* and *Cymbeline*.   The chief
early sceptic was the Italian humanist Polydore
Vergil, who worked at the court of Henry VII
and Henry VIII, and who applied to this mass
of legend the critical lessons he had learned
from ancient history.   During the 16th century,
however, Polydore was denounced by patriotic
historians; he was a delirious foreigner who
with one dash of a pen had cashiered threescore
princes together.   But moralists came to doubt

the glory of descent from "Venus, that lascivious adulteress,"[3] and the whole structure of legend was undermined by such sophisticated students of history as William Camden and John
Selden. Yet the poet Michael Drayton could
utter a wistful sigh for the tales "Which now the
envious world doth slander for a dream,"[4] and
Milton could salute the nymph of the Severn as

> Virgin, daughter of Locrine,
> Sprung of old Anchises' line.[5]

Henceforth, however, British history, sadly
shortened, was to begin with the bald, unroman-
tic figure of Julius Caesar.

There are many examples, in many areas, of
the growth of the historical spirit. The medieval man was likely to see his cherished Latin
authors rather as names attached to wise or en-
tertaining books than as men who lived in particular places in particular times; and he might
see Tullius and Cicero as two persons. The development of an historical consciousness — and
of aesthetic discrimination — was of course one
of the great marks of the Renaissance mind, and
it showed itself in Petrarch. Two generations
after Petrarch we meet such an exemplar of mature and active classical scholarship as Lau-
rentius or Lorenzo Valla, who not only put the
study of Latin style and idiom on a new basis
but turned his acutely critical learning upon
momentous documents: he proved that the Do-

nation of Constantine, which had long buttressed
papal claims to temporal power, was a forgery,
and he assigned to a date much later than the
apostolic age that rich source of medieval and
Renaissance Neoplatonism that went under the
name of Dionysius the Areopagite. Valla also
made the first scholarly criticism of errors in the
Latin Vulgate, in notes which Erasmus later
published. Erasmus, the greatest of all popu-
larizers of classical *humanitas* and "the philosophy of Christ," paid tribute to Valla and urged
the necessity of applying scholarship to sacred
as well as other texts. His edition in 1516 of the
Greek New Testament was an act of courage no
less than of religious and scholarly zeal, since
for over a thousand years the Latin Vulgate had
been in official use as virtually the word of God
himself. And one might add here the name of
John Colet, the friend of Erasmus and More,
Dean of St. Paul's and founder of St. Paul's
School. Colet was no classical humanist, but he
had studied in Italy and had some new light;
and while the professor of divinity at Oxford
lectured on Duns Scotus, Colet lectured there on
St. Paul's epistles. Though his main purpose
was naturally interpretation and application, he
treated the epistles, not as parts of an anonymous
and timeless (and allegorical) Bible, but as letters written by a certain man in a certain historical milieu.

As for the theory and practice of historical

writing, it was the ancients who taught that. By the 16th century the Roman historians, and the Greek historians in Latin versions, were available, and, as the century went on, both Romans and Greeks were put into the modern languages (sometimes by circuitous routes, as in Thomas Nicolls' English translation of a French translation of Valla's Latin translation of Thucydides). As a result, historiography entered upon a new era. Chronicles and world-histories on the medieval pattern continued to be written and read, but these gradually gave way to more sophisticated histories whose authors had profited from the ancients. The methods, if not the genius, of the classical historians, which a very few medieval writers had approached, became in time more general — the rejection of the fabulous and improbable, the use of documents, the weighing of evidence, the analysis of cause and effect, the effort toward coherent philosophical interpretation of characters and events. Early representatives of the new outlook and method were Machiavelli and Guicciardini. Machiavelli is perhaps not, either as man or as thinker, very attractive, but one much-quoted passage from a letter, written when he had been dismissed from his official post and was occupied on his small estate, shows the classical humanist in a gracious light:

> At nightfall I return home and seek my writing room, and, divesting myself on its threshold of my

rustic garments, stained with mud and mire, I assume
courtly attire, and thus suitably clothed, enter within the ancient courts of ancient men, by whom, being cordially welcomed, I am fed with the food that
alone is mine, and for which I was born, and am not
ashamed to hold discourse with them, and inquire the
motives of their actions; and these men in their humanity reply to me, and for the space of four hours
I feel no weariness, remember no trouble, no longer
fear poverty, no longer dread death; my whole being
is absorbed in them.[6]

Although in his chief work Machiavelli drew
political lessons for his own time from the pages
of Livy, he had much less affinity with that mel-
low *laudator temporis acti* than with the shrewd-
ly analytical and cynical Tacitus. In the 16th
and 17th centuries Tacitus was esteemed the
very bible of statesmen and, in addition to being
a model, for anti-Ciceronians, of concise and
epigrammatic style, he had a large share in
creating a mundane and realistic view of history. Bacon's *Henry VII* was one product of
that school. On the other hand there was a less
readily definable but more idealistic theory of
history which had distinctively medieval as
well as classical roots. For many writers and
readers of the Renaissance, as in earlier times,
history was not the analysis of power politics,
in the world or within the state, but ethical philosophy teaching by examples, a panorama of
God's judgments upon rulers and empires. It
was largely in that spirit, though not without

elements of "realism," that Sir Walter Ralegh
wrote his *History of the World,* and his religious vision inspired some noble and impas-
sioned meditations on the greatness and the lit-
tleness of man.   We might try to imagine, on the
page of a modern social scientist, a parallel to
this half-medieval, half-classical prose poem on
life and death,

> towards which we always travel both sleeping and
> waking: neither have those beloved companions of
> honor and riches any power at all, to hold us any one
> day, by the promises of glorious entertainments; but
> by what crooked path soever we walk, the same lead-
> eth on directly to the house of death, whose doors
> lie open at all hours, and to all persons.   For this
> tide of man's life, after it once turneth and declineth,
> ever runneth with a perpetual ebb and falling stream,
> but never floweth again: our leaf once fallen, spring-
> eth no more, neither doth the sun or the summer
> adorn us again, with the garments of new leaves and
> flowers.[7]

If we, like Matthew Arnold, are disturbed by
Ralegh's speculations about the site of paradise
and other problems which would have been
impossible for the critical mind of Thucydides,
we might remember, for instance, that Jerome
Cardan, the eminent Italian scientist of the
previous generation, held that a city's political
power would be great if the tail of the Great
Bear were vertical over it (a view attacked by
the still more eminent Jean Bodin, who had his

own occult instincts).[8] And it might be added that something akin to the spirit of Ralegh's book has informed a massive work of our age, Toynbee's *Study of History* — to the distress of "pure" historians and rationalistic liberals.

If we had time, we could follow up a similar double strain in the art of biography. For writers and readers who favored the realistic kind of history, there was such a biographical model as Suetonius' lives of the Roman emperors, which were put into English by the great translator of the early 17th century, Philemon Holland. For the more orthodox believer in ethical examples, there was Plutarch, who for centuries held a high place in the reading of old and young. Plutarch had the good fortune to be turned into felicitous French by Amyot and from French into the still more felicitous English of Sir Thomas North. The power of North's translation is not merely a matter of word and rhythm; it arises from a feeling that he shared with other men of the age, a reverence for the special greatness of ancient heroes combined with an instinctive sense of contemporaneous intimacy. Hence he ranges freely from the colloquial and slangy to the poetic, and on all levels he is dramatic. As everyone knows, North received the finest of tributes in having some passages, such as the description of Cleopatra's barge, taken over by Shakespeare with little more change than was needed to put them into verse.

We have looked, briefly, at two fields of
knowledge and have seen something of the ancient critical spirit in operation. We took science as one example because it might be too
readily assumed that that kind of knowledge developed altogether independently. But it was
the humanities, history (which was not yet a
social science), philosophy, and literature that
were most deeply rooted in ancient wisdom.
These liberal studies, *litterae humaniores,* were
concerned with man as man, as a rational and
ethical being and not as a professional or tech-
nical specialist. While the universities largely
maintained their scholastic and professional
curricula (though these were modified by humanism), education in the schools of Europe
was pretty thoroughly classical. Teachers of
the Renaissance period were far more numerous and better equipped than their medieval
predecessors, and they had the whole extant
body of classical literature to use, but the basic
aim of Renaissance education might still have
been summed up in the words of the twelfth-
century John of Salisbury, "the knowledge of
virtue that makes a good man."[9] We may recall
the similar utterances of Erasmus and Vives and
Roger Ascham and Milton and many other
men. Everywhere in the dozens of Renaissance
treatises on education we find the twin ideal,
virtue and good letters. It might of course be
said that the enunciation of such ideals only

corresponded to our Commencement Day addresses; that, since thousands of teachers cannot all be geniuses, there was much uninspired gerund-grinding; and that in many schoolrooms the only active Muse was "Lady Birch." Still, when we have made allowance for such human frailties, and for practical, professional motives behind the study of Latin, there remains ample evidence that in all the literary countries there was an extraordinary number of notable teachers, many of them writers too, and that — as Rabelais' Gargantua[10] and many other witnesses attest — there was an extraordinary enthusiasm for good letters, very often for virtue as well.

I should like to mention one example, an admittedly special example, of the realization in actual life of classical-Christian ideals. Perhaps the greatest Italian teacher of the earlier 15th century was Vittorino da Feltre. He labored with such zeal, piety, and gaiety in his all-embracing role as teacher of Latin and Greek, spiritual guide, athletic director, and nurse, that he was not, as we grimly say, a productive scholar; his life was given to his pupils. But one of those pupils happened to be the Federigo who became ruler of the little principality of Urbino. Under Federigo and his son Urbino was renowned, even in Renaissance Italy, as a center of the finest culture, and it remains famous because it was mirrored in the finest of all courtesy books, *The Courtier* of

Castiglione. Castiglione, a minor diplomat, was himself an ideal gentleman, versed in literature and painting, a poet and a friend of artists and writers, and no one could set forth with fuller authority the attributes of the ideal gentleman and amateur who, in addition to public service, makes life itself an art. Thus in a book partly based on Cicero's *De Oratore* — one of the half-dozen ancient treatises that created the formative ideals of Renaissance education — we have pictured an aristocratic group whose way of life was the flower of humanistic teaching. If the word "aristocratic" offends some ears, it may be said that Vittorino, who had been poor himself, took in as pupils poor boys who could not pay fees, that this kind of aristocratic education was being given to all and sundry in the thousands of European grammar schools (such as that in Stratford on Avon), and that education was conceived of in terms of the highest, not the lowest, common denominator.

During the Renaissance and well through the 19th century, all students all over Europe were brought up on the same body of literature, and study of that literature meant a unified literary, historical, political, ethical, and metaphysical knowledge and understanding. It is impossible to exaggerate the significance of the fact that all educated men, including scientists, held the classical heritage in common; that they had, or at any rate started from, a common experience and outlook, and were united by a uniform and universal bond of solidarity stronger in some ways than such dividing forces as the Reformation and rising nationalism. I do not mean that all men thought alike; the classics could be invoked, as we shall partly see, to support political or ethical or religious orthodoxy and also democratic or sceptical or naturalistic rebellion. But there was a broad highway that all men traveled, and both those who stayed on it and those who departed from it knew where they were going.

The importance of such a universal tradition we should be qualified to appreciate, after many decades of a chaotic elective system and vastly expanded curriculum. In his *Three Centuries of Harvard,* Professor Morison says that "Mr. Eliot, more than any other man, is responsible for the greatest educational crime of the century against American youth — depriving him of his classical heritage."[11] Of late years our colleges have been trying to install some kind of backbone among the floating ribs, appendixes, and adipose tissue of education; and in the world at large much earnest study has been given to problems of communication among widely different cultural groups and nations. The same problem of heterogeneous diversity of knowledge and outlook is conspicuously illustrated in modern poetry. In contrast with the private symbolism of so much modern writing, a Renaissance poet anywhere in Europe could assume in his readers a common stock of knowledge and for the most part a common outlook, and he could draw freely upon the traditional and international gold reserve. If the gold sometimes turned into brass, the same thing may happen to the most original private symbols.

A related fact or attitude, also traditional and international, was the conception of imaginative literature and its function. Fifty years ago Spingarn began his well-known book with the statement that "The first problem of Renaissance criticism was the justification of imaginative literature."[12] Throughout the Middle Ages, and the Renaissance as well, Plato's objections to poetry were recurrently fortified by Christian objections to pagan and often immoral writings. These Platonic and patristic and "puritan" complaints were met, during the Middle Ages and not seldom in the Renaissance, by the doctrine of allegorical truth contained beneath the husk of fiction. This allegorical and defensive method of exegesis, which had been practised in Greece before Plato, was later applied to both the Bible and the classics, notably the *Aeneid* and even the more doubtful poetry of Ovid; and it was given a popular restatement for the Renaissance by Boccaccio. Aristotle's *Poetics,* which was rediscovered about 1500, in time raised this and other fundamental questions to a new level. Plato's ethical objection to poetry, that it stirred

up harmful emotions, was countered by Aristotle's theory of catharsis (however that theory
might be interpreted) ; and Plato's metaphysical objection was invalidated by Aristotle's doctrine of ideal imitation, that art was not two
removes from truth, since it was a rendering,
not of the particular, but of the universal and
probable.   Thus the Aristotelian aesthetic established imaginative literature on a firm foundation.   In England, as elsewhere, moralists
could still complain, and the allegorical conception remained strong, but Sir Philip Sidney
at least could take his stand on Aristotelian imitation — and could also marshal Platonic arguments on behalf of poetry against Platonic
objections. However, poetry owed perhaps as
much to the allegorical tradition as to Aristotle.

The gradual change brought about by the
circulation of Aristotelian ideas did not appar-
ently weaken the ethical view of poetry that pre-
vailed in the Renaissance.   Aristotle's own view
of poetry was indeed essentially ethical.   And
when we think not merely of Plato and Aristotle
but of Aristophanes and Horace and Plutarch
and others, we may say that in antiquity the accepted function of literature was the making of
good men and good citizens.   To say that is not
to say that writers were all or always didactic,
or that the ethical conception meant preaching
or in any way detracted from the qualities that
belong to great writing; the place that the

Greeks and Romans have held in world literature is sufficient reassurance on that point. The
idea of delightful teaching was strongly rein-
forced in the Renaissance; through the imagi-
nation and emotions men might be stirred to the
active love of public and private virtue. For
serious humanists in the 16th century, as in the
12th, even the ancient writers of licentious comedy and satire contained moral instruction,
somewhat obliquely presented, and the philosophers — Plato, Cicero, and Seneca in particular
— had, through the limited but divine light of
natural reason, come close to Christian ideals of
righteousness. On the fusion of pagan wisdom
with Christianity one could quote countless
moving testimonies, from some of the Church
Fathers onward to Petrarch and Erasmus and
many English authors from Sir Thomas Elyot
to Milton. Not all humanists and imaginative
writers, to be sure, were conspicuous for virtue
or religion, since the classical revival, especially
in Italy and France, had its neopagans. But no
one who has hearkened to the cloud of witnesses
on the other side can doubt either the sincerity
of their ethical creed or the strength that much
of the greatest Renaissance writing derived
from it.

So far we have been concerned with the critical spirit of antiquity as it worked in the field of
knowledge, and with some central principles of
education and literary theory. In the next chap-

ter we shall go on for a bit with poetic theory
and then look more directly at literature itself
and at classical influence upon form, style, and
content; and that will include the clash as well
as the fusion of pagan and Christian ideas.

II

WE MIGHT as well admit, some time, that when we use the word "classical" in a broad sense, we don't as a rule have a very clear notion of what we mean. We may say, quite truly, that the word applies to such writers as Molière and Racine, Milton and Jane Austen, and that it does not apply to such writers as Blake and Shelley and Whitman and D. H. Lawrence. And perhaps that leaves us wiser. If we want more direct criteria and survey the Greek writers from Homer to Theocritus or Lucian, we have considerable trouble in naming qualities of outlook and style that are common to all alike. The effort may not get beyond some such answer as "Centrality, sanity, and concrete clarity of vision and expression, focused upon the actualities of human nature and life, and not blurred or softened by the refractions which, in modern literature, are associated with sentimentalism, romanticism, and other aberrations." And that, even if acceptable, is not very usable.

But the word "classical" covers the Romans as well as the Greeks, and if we check our definition in the light of Latin literature from Lucretius and Catullus to Tacitus and Martial, we must bring in so many positive or negative modifications that we are further still from a uniform and usable criterion. We may agree on the solid initial fact that Roman literature in general, compared with the Greek, was itself "neoclassical," since it embodied many of the formal and rhetorical elements which the modern period of so-called neoclassicism greatly prized and carried to frequent excess. Moreover, the Middle Ages, the Renaissance, and the neoclassical age were nourished preponderantly on Latin literature and usually regarded it as the standard. It is, by the way, one of the signal proofs of Dryden's critical discernment and candor that, at the height of the neoclassical age in England, he could contrast Chaucer's forthright naturalness of apprehension and expression with Ovid's incessant rhetorical tricks and see the medieval poet as a more truly classical writer than the ancient.[1] Not, we may add, that Chaucer was a naive or uneducated poet, or unaware of medieval and Ovidian rhetoric; but his mature vision was focused directly on the object and the idea. All this is only an elaborate warning that neoclassicism was often unclassical, and that the greatest writers of the Renaissance — including the greatest of English classicists, Milton — were, happily, not altogether classicized. If, in the ensuing discussion, an undue amount of evidence is taken from English literature, it is partly because the writer is not a universal doctor and partly because the limitation of space favors the use of what is most generally familiar.

Men of the Renaissance had a profound reverence for the ancient poets, philosophers, orators, statesmen, and heroes as a superior race, and this was a dynamic faith, not a genteel tradition. As modern literature and science and civilization developed, progressives might deny any such inherent superiority and set up the moderns against the ancients, but that note of protest was seldom heard before 1600. The true spirit of veneration and imitation was expressed by such a bold intelligence as Valla, in the preface to his work on Latin style. In the place of the old Roman empire, he says, there remains the universal sway of the Roman language, in which are contained all the disciplines worthy of a free man: when the language flourishes, all branches of knowledge flourish, and when it dies, they die; for who have been the great thinkers, orators, jurists, authors, if not those men who have striven most studiously to speak well? More than a century after Valla, the same faith was stated with even simpler piety by Thomas Wilson in his *Art of Rhetoric:*

> Now before we use either to write or speak eloquently, we must dedicate our minds wholly to follow the most wise and learned men, and seek to fashion as well their speech and gesturing as their wit or inditing. The which when we earnestly mind to do, we cannot but in time appear somewhat like them.[2]

Such imitative zeal could of course lead to wrongheadedness. The sometimes extravagant

worship and imitation of Cicero's style drew a
famous satire from Erasmus and a famous censure from Bacon, who saw the study of words
instead of matter as one of the main obstacles in
the way of progress. On the other hand, Cicero
was in fact not only the chief creator of modern
prose style but the chief ethical teacher and civi-
lizer of Europe; and Erasmus, while he sati-
rized misguided and frivolous Ciceronianism,
was himself a reverent admirer of the almost
Christian moralist. It might be said further
that Bacon was really attacking the whole tradition of humanistic education, with much the
same prejudices as John Dewey's, and that the
great humanists did not put words before matter.
Their matter was the nature of man and society,
and they were wisely conscious of the relations
between style and the general pattern of ethical
and social order. We may say of them what Mr.
Trilling has said of that authentic later humanist, Matthew Arnold, that whenever he talks
about style he is talking about society.[3] If we
are sceptical concerning such a relationship,
there is an obvious answer in the parallel between the state of the modern world and the
modern soul and the more disordered manifesta-
tions of literary and pictorial art.

Sir Philip Sidney, the first important English
classicist, supplies another example of wrongheadedness, if one may use so harsh a word, in
the manly and winning revelation of a conflict

between his natural instincts and his formal creed:

> Certainly I must confess my own barbarousness, I never heard the old song of Percy and Douglas that I found not my heart moved more than with a trumpet, and yet is it sung but by some blind crowder, with no rougher voice than rude style; which, being so evil appareled in the dust and cobwebs of that uncivil age, what would it work, trimmed in the gorgeous eloquence of Pindar?[4]

One danger in Renaissance classicism — especially as the art of the poet was associated with that of the orator — was a tendency to forget that style and form are inward and integral elements of writing, not a rhetorical vesture and pattern imposed from without; but this was a weakness of minor rather than major writers. More special diseases came out in the kind of verbal and rhetorical rash represented by such labels as Petrarchianism, Euphuism, Gongorism, and Marinism; and even the greatest writers, from Shakespeare down, might be infected. Yet these excesses cannot simply be ascribed to ancient influence, and a fundamental — and ultimately successful — aim of neoclassicism was to curb eccentricity and achieve a rational, civilized norm of expression. The lengths to which neoclassical concern for stylistic decorum could go were epigrammatically summed up in George Brandes' remark about Voltaire, that the man who respected little in heaven or earth respected the uniform caesura.[5]

The formal literary creed of the Renaissance was an amalgam of Aristotle and Horace and others, fused and reinterpreted by theorists and practitioners in terms of their own age and country. Though there was emphasis on the emotive power of poetry, the creed tended to operate on a practical level, to convert suggestive principles into a code of rules. The most familiar example is the crystallization of Aristotle's basic doctrine of unity of dramatic action, along with his more casual reference to the customary limit of time, into the three unities of action, time, and place. The authority of the unities was not broken until the 18th century. But "the rules" were always much stronger in France, the Gallic mind being disposed toward order and decorum, than in England, where the national genius was not so disposed and where Shakespeare remained one powerful solvent. In Renaissance Europe at large, it should be added, the hardening of the rules was at least checked by two perennial sources of fire, the Platonic conception of poetic "enthusiasm" and the treatise on the sublime that goes under the name of Longinus.

It was the formalistic habit of mind that translated or perverted the Aristotelian doctrine of imitation of nature, of life, into imitation of ancient authors, whose imitations of life were by common consent the supreme models. This theory of literary imitation had, to be sure, originated in antiquity, but it remained a fairly moderate and judicious precept until the Renaissance made it a prime article in the neoclassical creed. It was expounded, for instance in Vida's *Art of Poetry* in the early 16th century and in Pope's *Essay on Criticism* in the early 18th. Virgil, says Pope, planned to draw the *Aeneid* wholly from nature,

> But when t' examine ev'ry part he came,
> Nature and Homer were, he found, the same.
> Convinc'd, amaz'd, he checks the bold design;
> And rules as strict his labour'd work confine,
> As if the Stagirite o'erlooked each line.
> Learn hence for ancient rules a just esteem;
> To copy Nature is to copy them.

Obviously such a theory was in danger of encouraging academic reproductions of the antique, not expressions of human experience. On the other hand, such a theory, wisely followed, inculcated a beneficial consciousness of great materials and great form and style; it meant that writers and readers were aware of tradition, of the principles of decorum governing the various genres, of controlling standards above individual vagaries and fashions of the moment.*

---

*To mention a minute and casual item in Mr. Gilbert Highet's big and excellent book, *The Classical Tradition,* when he (p. 110) applies the word "false" to Milton's description of Shakespeare warbling his native wood-notes wild, he forgets the principle of decorum: Milton naturally takes the outdoor comedies as the appropriate reading of the mirthful man. He is also, of course, contrasting the unlearned Shakespeare with the learned Jonson.

Such ideas and attitudes are as far removed from those of our time as Renaissance education is, and they might disconcert a reader who was wholly conditioned by modern theory and practice. The modern writer cares nothing for genres and is likely to associate convention with stereotypes — though the reader of *Lycidas,* for instance, knows how greatly a great poet can work in and through a convention. The modern poet and reader assume that poetry must be written in the language and rhythms of common speech; the Renaissance poet and reader would accept that doctrine for satire but would expect most other kinds of poetry to be distinctly poetical. The modern writer and reader, while abhorring didacticism, expect a poem to be a revelation of the author's state of mind, to be, that is, a disillusioned comment on life. The Renaissance writer and reader normally held a firm belief in the ethical function of poetry and at the same time wrote and treasured lovely pieces of jeweled artifice that told little about the poet and less about life; and in neither case was self-expression regarded as the end. These are a few rapid and unqualified contrasts, but they may serve their purpose.

We have noted some virtues of Renaissance education and literary theory, and have admitted also the danger, for a writer, of over-education — which is not the commonest danger in our time. An educated writer of the Renaissance, though he was a man living in his own world, having his own experience, could not simply look in his heart, or around him, and write. He was himself so eagerly responsive to literary tradition, and critical authority was so busy in the necessary task of ordering and refining form and style, that only an original mind could keep his balance. But if, for instance, we are deaf to the muffled sound and fury of the hundreds of academic Senecan dramas, the fashion may be said to have been justified by such a non-academic product as *Hamlet*. In other words, the greatest writers of the Renaissance were those who, granted their special genius, could profit from the classics without becoming sedulous apes, and without losing their own fresh vision of life or their contact with native and popular elements of tradition.

That is doubtless a truism, but, for a varied array of illustrious examples, consider such men as Ariosto, Tasso, Camoens, Spenser, Rabelais, and Cervantes. The first four represent the heroic poem, which the Renaissance, in its general exaltation of classical genres, put at the top. Petrarch's unfinished but ambitiously cherished *Africa* was the first of the scores of neoclassical epics which were to litter the 16th, 17th, and 18th centuries and of which only one transcendent work survives, *Paradise Lost*. But the four poets just mentioned, though influenced by the classics, were not strict neoclassicists in method

or style. Ariosto, going back to the romances of
Charlemagne and chivalry, which Boiardo had
lately handled, created a lively and brilliant
panoramic narrative, at once idealistic and
ironical. The Italian critics were much exercised over the question whether the *Orlando
Furioso,* with its fluid episodic structure and
numerous heroes and heroines, was an epic or a
romance; but some reached the sage conclusion
that, if Aristotle could have read it, he would
have approved. Half a century later, at the
time of Lepanto, the serious Tasso turned to the
Crusades for material and, rendered more conscious of problems of form, made a more unified
but still highly romantic poem. Spenser, hoping
to "overgo" the Italians, and linking them as
ethical teachers with Homer and Virgil, like-
wise used the materials of chivalry, folklore,
and the supernatural, all informed by the desire
to "fashion a gentleman or noble person in ver-
tuous and gentle discipline."⁶ Spenser drew
upon a wide range of ancient, medieval, and
modern literature, Platonic and Aristotelian
ethics, Ovid and Virgil, medieval romances and
the Italian heroic poems. Finally, Camoens
achieved success in what might have seemed an
impossible feat; he made the relatively recent
voyage of Vasco da Gama the theme of a Portu-
guese epic, with celestial machinery taken from
classical myth. What gave life to these poems
was not merely the use of national history or

legend (which neoclassical theory and ancient practice prescribed), but originality, vigor, and eclecticism that went far beyond imitation. On the other hand Ronsard, the prince of sixteenth-century French lyrists, felt impelled to write a national epic, and declared, with unconscious irony, that, unless his readers knew the ancients well, his poem would be a dead weight in their hands.[7] Like so many things of its kind, it was a dead weight anyhow.

As for the two great men of prose, Rabelais, a classical humanist and medical scientist, is no exemplar of neoclassical decorum; he carried the Paul-Bunyanesque giant-lore of popular tradition to a new level of uproarious humor, satire, and *joie de vivre*. The more sober Cervantes can hardly, any more than Shakespeare, be grouped with scholarly writers — though a recent critic remarks that his "discovery of Aristotle, even at second or third hand, with the revelation that literature had its own body of precept, its rules, was the great aesthetic experience of his life"[8]— but Cervantes was, like Shakespeare, a great interpreter of man who was not diverted from the popular by neoclassicism. On the other hand, we may think that Cervantes' profound sanity and irony, like Shakespeare's, would not be what they are if his age had not been tempered by classical rationality. At the same time, thinking of ancient comedy, we might add that other qualities in

Cervantes and Shakespeare, the clear recognition of good and evil, the sympathetic understanding of human idealism and human folly,
were possible only in a civilization leavened by
Christianity.

In this general connection we cannot very well
avoid the conventional, not to say threadbare,
contrast between Shakespeare and Jonson,
though Shakespeare was not the mere child of
nature of many early eulogies and though Jonson was not a mere neoclassicist. When we
compare their dramatizations of Roman history,
it is obvious that Shakespeare exercised his un-
trammeled intuition upon the characters and
data of North's *Plutarch* and heightened the
vivid contemporaneous immediacy already present in the translation; whereas Jonson, with the
historical conscience of a scholar, enveloped
Sejanus and Catiline in speeches more studiously
composed out of Cicero, Sallust, Tacitus, and
scholarly commentaries. Jonson's powers found
of course their chief expression in comedy, and
here he had before him classical comedy and
satire and the precepts of Horace and modern
critics. Some of Shakespeare's romantic comedies had a remote classical ancestry, since pas-
toral romances of the Renaissance were derived
from late Greek and medieval romance, but the
world of Arden, Illyria, and Bohemia had little
to do with relentless satire of urban manners and
morals, of knaves and gulls.

There is a similar typical difference in the two poets' lyrics. Shakespeare's, though not naive, have an air of spontaneous ease and a clear affinity with popular song — and so do some of Jonson's. But some of Jonson's most characteristic pieces, such as "Drink to me only with thine eyes," come from classical sources and show the conscious contrivance, the intellectualized pattern and style, of a scholarly poet. For example, take their handling of the ancient theme of *Carpe diem,* on which hundreds of Renaissance poets rang all possible changes over and over again. In "O mistress mine, where are you roaming?" the theme is classical and its development is strictly logical, but we forget all that in hearing a simple, innocent, tuneful ditty from a timeless Arcadia. As soon as we begin Jonson's

> Come, my Celia, let us prove,
> While we may, the sports of love,

we know that we are intended to enjoy a light adaptation of Catullus, a picture of the sophisticated game of love as played in ancient Rome or modern London. But all these obvious remarks are by way of distinction, not disparagement of the lesser poet. Jonson was much too fine an artist, and much too tough-minded an observer of life, to reveal more than traces of the pedantry of neoclassicism. For him, as for other independent writers, the ancients were "Guides, not Commanders."[9]

We may turn to one or two representative
classical themes which were treated in lyric and
heroic poem, in prose tale and drama. None
was more central in the tradition than the story
of Troy, and none illustrates better the infinite
poetic value of a malleable body of myth that is
a universal inheritance. A modern poet who
wished to deal with the subject would read
Homer, or at any rate Lang, Leaf, and Myers.
Some Renaissance poets knew Greek, and all
knew the Trojan parts of Virgil and Ovid, but
many used, and few were unaffected by, the very
un-Homeric mixture of epic and romance that
the Middle Ages built upon a rough ancient
foundation. Every student of literature, or at
least every candidate for the Ph.D., knows the
outline of the long process that began with the
prosaic and circumstantial narratives of Dares
and Dictys, the medieval substitutes for Homer.
The large and romantic elaborations of these
tales were not products of "medieval naiveté;"
they were sophisticated modernizations of the
kind begun by Ovid, the chief progenitor of
courtly love, and often written in our time. For
Englishmen of the Elizabethan age the standard
popular version of the Trojan story was the
prose romance translated from the French by
Caxton, a version which, by the way, continued
to be printed up into the 18th century.

One offshoot of this tradition became, especially in England, almost as conspicuous as the

parent stem, that is, the wholly medieval story
of Troilus, Cressida, and Diomede. The story
was first developed in the Old French *Romance
of Troy,* of the 12th century, and was widely
known through the Latin prose version of that
work. It was expanded by Boccaccio, who drew
upon his own experience as well as literary
sources. Following Boccaccio, Chaucer re-
created the characters and their significance
with all his own humor, dramatic power, sympathetic insight, and tragic irony. The world
of his great poem or novel of courtly love is of
course not Homeric but chivalric; Chaucer's
vision of realities was not obstructed by a concern for archaeology. Then the Scottish Chau-
cerian, Robert Henryson, wrote a short and
moving sequel in which the faithless Cressida
sank to painful degradation; in the 16th century
this poem was commonly read as Chaucer's and
it had a large share in fixing the popular notion
of the heroine. Finally Shakespeare, whether
experiencing a dark mood of cynicism or ex-
perimenting in the acrid Jonsonian vein of
satire, made his dramatic version in which traditional ideals of love and honor are corroded
by the poisons of "war and lechery." We need
not go on to Dryden's play.

This brief sketch is a reminder that the classical revival did not mean that Renaissance
writers and readers outlawed pseudo-classical
inventions and intermediaries and gave them-

selves exclusively to the authentic classics.
There was no reason why they should have done
so, since the themes of literature are not a matter of historical purism; and ancient literature
itself had been a long series of similar accretions
and variations. One side of this question must
have a word more. Recent scholarship has been
revealing to what an unexpected — and yet altogether natural — degree even learned writers
of the Renaissance made use of dictionaries of
mythology, a practice that to some people may
carry a suggestion of the second-hand and
cheap. But, since all poets had some classical
education and a feeling for antiquity, it made
small difference where an immediate hint came
from. And the importance of handbooks of
myth, such as those of Boccaccio and Natalis
Comes and Cartari, was not merely that they
fulfilled the function of similar modern books,
but still more that they gave allegorical and
ethical interpretations. It was no less legitimate
and fruitful, for such well-educated poets as
Spenser and Chapman and even the learned
Jonson, to use such works than it was for Mr.
Eliot to use *The Golden Bough.*

Wherever poets got their inspiration, it was,
as I said before, of immeasurable value that they
and their readers should share a traditional, international, and inexhaustibly varied treasury of
myth and symbol. Such symbols could become
meaningless counters, but they have always been

fresh when felt freshly. For one famous, simple, and magical example, that slangy Elizabethan journalist, Thomas Nashe, could create such an atmosphere that one name calls up all the associations of glamorous youth and beauty and love, and age and death:

> Beauty is but a flower
> Which wrinkles will devour;
> Brightness falls from the air,
> Queens have died young and fair,
> Dust hath closed Helen's eye.
> I am sick, I must die.
>   Lord, have mercy on us!

And with that must be linked a no less familiar and magical evocation:

> Was this the face that launched a thousand ships,
> And burnt the topless towers of Ilium?
> Sweet Helen, make me immortal with a kiss.

If we ask why — apart from the poets' expressive power — these classical allusions are so moving, one answer is that they crystallize the conflict between paganism and medieval Christianity. Nashe, in the time of the plague, sees the most beautiful of women against the background of *"Ubi sunt . . .?"* and the Dance of Death. And neither Dr. Faustus, the very symbol of Renaissance *hybris,* nor Marlowe, who has often been called that, can escape from God. Faustus' vision of an immortality of the senses is a contrivance of the devil; and later, when he must surrender his soul and time will not stand

still, his delusive ecstasy is recalled by the use
of the Ovidian Aurora's cry to the horses of the
night to check their gallop and prolong her
joys. But then his agonized vision is of Christ's
blood streaming in the firmament, God's ireful
brows, and immortality in hell.

Classical myth was not always treated with
such poignant brevity. But we shall pass by the
innumerable and richly decorative versions of
myths and tales which were written in Italy,
France, Spain, and England, and of which the
best-known specimens are *Hero and Leander*
and *Venus and Adonis*. In such poems the
sensuous or the sensual might be an end in itself,
or it might embody a philosophic theme. The
same thing may be said of the mythological allusions which are everywhere in Renaissance
writing. Ovid's *Metamorphoses,* the most popular ancient storehouse of both tales and allusions, was itself highly pictorial. Renaissance
poets, led by the Italians, went far beyond Ovid,
and beyond medieval Ovidians like Chaucer, in
pictorial elaboration and sensuous warmth and
color. One general reason, amply illustrated in
contemporary Italian painting, was a new, and
what used to be called "pagan," recognition of
the beauties of art and nature and the human
body. A weighty theoretical sanction was provided by the doctrine *"ut pictura poesis."* This
doctrine, originally a compound of ideas and
phrases from Simonides, Aristotle, Horace, and

Plutarch, made poetry a speaking picture and painting silent poetry. That is, a poet should with words create the effect of the painter's brush and pigments. To poets rediscovering the world of the senses, it was a congenial creed, and it lasted up to Lessing and beyond. To take one example, Ovid, describing the pictures woven by Arachne, says simply that "she made Leda lying under the wings of the swan." Spenser, describing the tapestries in the house of Busyrane, gives a whole stanza to the scene:

> Then was he turnd into a snowy Swan,
>   To win faire Leda to his lovely trade:
>   O wondrous skill, and sweet wit of the man,
>   That her in daffadillies sleeping made,
>   From scorching heat her daintie limbes to shade:
>   Whiles the proud Bird ruffing his fethers wyde,
>   And brushing his faire brest, did her invade;
>   She slept, yet twixt her eyelids closely spyde,
> How towards her he rusht, and smiled at his pryde.[10]

The doctrine *"ut pictura poesis"* could of course encourage description for the sake of description, but the stanza quoted, like almost all such things in the most pictorial of poets, has a purpose; Spenser is illustrating, with appropriate "realism," the sensual attractions of courtly love.

One special and popular convention was the catalogue of the beauties of the female body. Here again there is a contrast between the medieval catalogue, comprehensive but cool, and the Renaissance catalogue, comprehensive and warm. This sort of description, starting from the Song of Songs, Anacreon, and Ovid, had an influential exponent in Ariosto, in his pictures of the sensual enchantress Alcina and of Angelica and Olympia, who were both, like Andromeda, bound naked to a rock. Among English poets who took over the convention were Thomas Watson (who named Ariosto as one of the sources of his "passion"[11]), Sir Philip Sidney, and Spenser. Spenser, in the *Amoretti* and *Epithalamion,* raised the tone of such catalogues above mere lusciousness. The *Epithalamion,* by the way, which I will venture to call the finest love poem in the language, is an example of Spenser's eclectic yet wholly individual quality. It is a wedding hymn in the tradition of Catullus and other Roman poets and their French imitators, in the form of a stately Italian canzone, a series of processional pictures with a mingling of Irish and mythological allusions, of Irish and Roman festivities, all wrought into a ritualistic offering worthy of the Christian marriage altar.

While Ovidian narratives and anatomical catalogues were outlets for neopaganism, Renaissance poets could be quite sincere and serious in using a similar technique to depict sensual temptation as the insidious foe of man's integrity and the heroic life. The great vehicle for that theme was inevitably the story of Circe. The moral implicit in Homer was recognized in antiquity and was made very explicit by such Renaissance interpreters of myth as Natalis Comes. In Renaissance poetry Circe's sisters and cousins, if not aunts, may be reckoned by the dozens. Even the light-hearted Ariosto, though normally no moralist, made Alcina's powers of seduction the occasion of a moral episode. Tasso's Armida and the luxurious sensuality of her abode gave some materials and ideas to Spenser, whose Bower of Bliss is for most of us the great example of the tradition. But the climax of Spenser's book of Temperance was far from a mere imitation of Tasso, partly because he fused together a varied abundance of related motifs, Homeric, medieval, and Italian, and still more because he made every item in the account of the Bower and its inmates contribute to the cumulative and overpowering picture of debilitated lust. Critics have often gone wrong about the Bower of Bliss, saying that for once the serious moralist has broken out of harness and let himself go in satisfying his essentially voluptuous temperament. But, since C. S. Lewis wrote on Spenser,[12] no one can fall into that error again. The poet followed two main lines of suggestion. One is emphasis on his favorite contrast between rich unwholesome artifice and simple healthy nature. Ivy, for instance, is made of gold colored to imitate real ivy, and even its branches partake of the character of the Bower — "Low his lascivious armes

adown did creepe."[13] The second line of suggestion is emphasis on the diseased sensuality which
enjoys only the perpetual and unsated lust of
the eye — represented by the strip-tease damsels
in the pool and by the Circean Acrasia — as op-
posed to the healthy, honorable love and fruition
symbolized in the Garden of Adonis[14] and especially in the representative of chastity and true
love, Britomart.   In contrast with the natural
health of the Garden, or Britomart's passionate
love for her future husband, the atmosphere of
Acrasia's Bower is heavy with corruption.   If,
by the way, we think of Spenser's characteristic
diffuseness as very far from classical conciseness
(or from the elliptical conciseness of parallel
episodes in *The Waste Land*), we should ask if
his desired effects could have been achieved
without aggregation and repetition.

This topic has brought us within reach of the
last thing we can discuss, the conflict, in and
behind much serious Renaissance literature, between orthodox Christian humanism and the
rising forces of scepticism and naturalism.   That
conflict is at the center of our subject because the
classics gave powerful support to both sides —
and, in somewhat altered terms, the conflict is
still with us.

The modern phrase "Christian humanism" is
a label for the medieval and Renaissance synthesis, the result of the long effort, which began
with some of the Church Fathers, to reconcile

and fuse the natural wisdom of the pagans with
the supernatural illumination of Christianity.
The first great philosophic system, that of
Aquinas, rested on the poles of divine and human reason. The Thomistic synthesis, however,
gave way to the voluntarism, represented by
William of Ockham, which made God not Absolute Reason but Absolute Will, a concept
which passed on to Luther and Calvin, with
all the added force of the Augustinian doctrine
of human depravity. The Christian humanists
of the Renaissance were more literary and practical, and less rigorously philosophical, than
the scholastics, and their ideal was the religion
of the New Testament instead of scholastic
logic, but they may be said to have inherited the
Thomistic impulse and attitude. The Renaissance philosophy of order, though not a *Summa*
built by any one mind, was a reassertion of the
rationality of God and the rational dignity and
free will of man — hence, for example, Erasmus' break with Luther. This mode of thought,
or view of life, attained its most coherent ma-
turity in the 17th century, with Milton and the
Cambridge Platonists, but most essentials were
set forth in the first book of Hooker's *Ecclesiastical Polity,* where he surveyed the reign of
law in the universe and in the mind of God and
man.

This philosophy of order has been described
rather often of late years and only a few head-

ings can be recalled now. The center and foundation was of course Christian faith and theology, with its conception of God and the nature and destiny of man. Then the whole universe, from God down to inanimate nature, is a hierarchy of being. It is the glory, and the peril, of man that he occupies a middle position, linked on the one hand with the angels and God, on the other with the beasts. He is endowed with a rational soul, which should rule over his appetites and passions as God rules over the forces of nature. What holds for the universe and the individual also holds for society, which is not a chaotic aggregate of individuals but a hierarchical organism in which everyone has his place and function. Thus the individual soul and society and the cosmos constitute one interrelated order. Perhaps the briefest and most eloquent summary is the sentence with which Hooker closes his first book:

> . . . Of Law there can be no less acknowledged, than that her seat is the bosom of God, her voice the harmony of the world: all things in heaven and earth do her homage, the very least as feeling her care, and the greatest as not exempted from her power, both angels and men and creatures of what condition soever, though each in different sort and manner, yet all with uniform consent, admiring her as the mother of their peace and joy.

There is no time to show how ethical, social, and metaphysical components of this doctrine were drawn from Aristotle, from Plato and Neoplatonism, and from the Stoicism of Cicero and Seneca. Nor is there time for more than one or two references to the way in which it conditioned or worked in imaginative literature. The *locus classicus* for some things is Ulysses' speech on "degree" in *Troilus and Cressida*,[15] a speech which has been related to Hooker and to Sir Thomas Elyot's *Governor* and which is at any rate good humanistic orthodoxy. But it is only one small and concrete illustration of the fact that the orthodox synthesis provided the underlying assumptions of Shakespeare's plays. If that assertion seems disputable, we have only to put him beside some modern naturalistic writers to realize that his characters speak, act, and are judged in relation to a philosophy of order, and are not merely observed with entire moral detachment or in a moral vacuum.

For more tangible evidence, we may glance at a poet and dramatist who, unlike Shakespeare, was an earnest crusader and, in a not altogether pejorative sense, a doctrinaire preacher. George Chapman's large borrowings, which he fused into a creed both typically humanistic and intensely personal, have been laid bare by scholarship, and the names of some principal creditors are significant — Epictetus, Plutarch, Marsilio Ficino, Erasmus, Natalis Comes.[16] In other words, Chapman is a Christian Stoic with a marked strain of Platonism. In his central poem,

The Tears of Peace, Chapman urges men to translate learning into active moral wisdom, the reason's control of the body's mutinous realm; that is "the rich crown of old Humanity." His tragedies about Bussy d'Ambois and Byron are dramatic presentations of passion and will running amuck, in contrast with the disciplined insight and self-control of the "Senecal man." Even in his noble version of Homer, whom he worshiped as the supreme poet and teacher, Chapman continually made explicit, sometimes with considerable additions to the text, the same conflict between reason and passion. I am rather given to quoting, from Chapman's preface to the *Odyssey,* a piece of fervent and eloquent Stoicism in which he is comparing Achilles with his great hero, Odysseus:

> In one, predominant perturbation; in the other, overruling wisdom; in one, the body's fervor and fashion of outward fortitude, to all possible height of heroical action; in the other, the mind's inward, constant, and unconquered empire, unbroken, unaltered, with any most insolent and tyrannous infliction.

That was the spirit in which Homer could be read, and we could hardly have more impressive testimony to reverence for ancient greatness and to the ethical function of poetry.

In England this philosophy of order commanded almost complete allegiance. Among writers, there was only an occasional rebel like the young John Donne, who in religion was not a sceptic (in the sense of unbeliever) but who in some moods enjoyed making witty and paradoxical arguments for sexual promiscuity. On the continent both religious scepticism and ethical naturalism had long been rising in strength; indeed these modes of thought were as old as their humanistic opposites, or older. Whereas Christian humanism carried on, from Plato and others, a belief in universal values sanctioned alike by God and by nature, God's instrument, scepticism, whether deistic or more radical, denied the Christian scheme, and naturalism, appealing to a different conception of "nature," denied the moral absolutes of classical and Christian thought. Even Cicero, the chief source of Renaissance humanism, was also, through his books on the nature of the gods and on divination, a source of sceptical and naturalistic arguments, which were used, for instance, by Rabelais and Montaigne. Other ancient solvents of orthodoxy were Lucretius, the passionate preacher of Epicurean materialism; Pliny, who acknowledged no God except Nature and saw man as inferior to animals in the struggle for survival; Lucian, the arch-mocker of all things sacrosanct; and Sextus Empiricus, who expounded the Pyrrhonist doctrine of the impossibility of knowledge. The Middle Ages contributed much to these streams of thought — Averroistic pantheism, Nominalism, which drove a wedge between reason and faith and

rejected universal abstractions in favor of the
particulars of experience, and the libertine
naturalism of such men as Jean de Meung, the
second author of the immensely popular *Romance of the Rose*. From the early 16th century onward, the "Aristotelian" rationalism of
Pomponazzi gained ground in Italy and spread
from there to France. Even the Reformation,
as the first great rebellion against religious authority, gave aid and comfort to much more
thoroughgoing rebels.

As one representative of scepticism and naturalism we may take the first and greatest of
modern essayists, Montaigne. When he began
his serious reading and writing, secluded in that
tower of his chateau which rose above household
bustle, Montaigne's search for an ethical philosophy led him in the Stoic direction. But a
man so responsive to life, so curious about human and especially his own nature, could not
dwell for long on the plane of Senecan austerity.
The influence of the more practical and flexible
Plutarch, the awakening of his instinctive inde-
pendence, and the discovery of Sextus Empiricus brought him to a second phase, represented
by the "Apology of Raymond Sebond." This
long essay, far from being a defence of natural
theology, turns into an exposition of Pyrrhonist
scepticism, a denial of the claims of the senses
and reason to attain truth and of the possibility
of human communication with ultimate reality.

But such scepticism was for Montaigne less of a weapon than a broom, a means of clearing the way to a working creed of relativism and naturalism. The Stoic maxim, "Follow Nature," which meant allying one's self with the collective "right reason" of mankind and the providential course of the world, has been translated into "Follow your own nature." Man cannot, says Montaigne, rise above himself (as Seneca had urged), except through religion, and he, though always a nominal Catholic, does not take much personal account of divine grace; he has neither an angel's nor a horse's conscience but a man's conscience, which is contented with itself. There were higher levels than that, and lower ones. Montaigne's was a discriminating and, up to a point, a fastidious nature which required intellectual and philosophic pleasures, and in his own way he was inclined toward order and tradition; for him, Alexander, who conquered the world, was a lesser man than Socrates, who led his life in conformity with nature — though Socrates might not have found Montaigne's creed quite satisfying. Thus Montaigne's influence was to support both conservatism and sceptical naturalism. He has been mentioned here as a supremely candid and disturbing questioner of accepted verities and pseudo-verities, who leaves aspiring man stripped, for good or ill, of many of his traditional supports and ideals.

These two antagonistic conceptions of life, both in a large degree classical, bring us into the modern world with all its conflicts and confusions, which since 1600 have been greatly heightened by science. We must stop here, though I should like to have mentioned other things. There are, for example, Spenser's *Cantos of Mutability,* in which the poet rises far above his Ovidian materials to present, or rather to admit, the painful struggle between his belief in a world evolving under divine providence and his vivid consciousness of a world of cruel strife and change. But to end with Shakespeare, as no doubt we should, we may say that by the time of the great tragedies the finest of minds, grown restless and sceptical, is able to question traditional beliefs, to entertain the idea of life as meaningless flux, and to probe the depths of evil, and yet he has not lost the traditional ideal of inward and outward order and faith in the actual or potential greatness and goodness of man.

Thus the briefest sketch of classical influence in Renaissance literature becomes a picture, not of a well quietly filling up with literary culture, but of many vigorous currents and whirlpools, literary and philosophical, scientific and religious. And one of many paradoxes is that the age which in literature and thought was zealously seeking order was also the age that saw the rise of modern naturalism. The naturalistic creed is now the natural creed of modern minds, who insist that no other view of life is possible — although we seem to hear less of the moral wisdom evolved by that creed than of laments for the breakdown of values. At any rate, however disheartening the spectacle of our civilization, the classics are still there as both a dynamic and a stabilizing force, and some of the chief writers of our century are proof of the continued vitality of the classical tradition.

NOTES

Since an adequate bibliography would take more space than the text, notes are restricted to some of the more direct references. Two general guides may be mentioned. One is Huntington Brown's "The Classical Tradition in English Literature: A Bibliography," *Harvard Studies and Notes in Philology and Literature,* XVIII (1935), 7-46. The other is Gilbert Highet's *The Classical Tradition: Greek and Roman Influences on Western Literature* (New York and London: Oxford University Press, 1949); this massive work (which appeared two years after these two lectures were given) devotes half a dozen chapters to the Renaissance and includes full bibliographical notes.

CHAPTER I

1. For the three quotations from Isidore of Seville, see his *Etymologiarum . . . Libri XX,* ed. W. M. Lindsay (Oxford Classical Texts), XII.vi.25, III.xlix, XI.i.127; and Ernest Brehaut, "An Encyclopedist of the Dark Ages: Isidore of Seville," *Studies in History, Economics and Public Law,* XLVIII (New York: Columbia University Press, 1912).

2. For Bacon's account of the diseases of learning, see *The Advancement of Learning, Works,* ed. Spedding, Ellis, and Heath (London, 1870-75), III, 282 f.; for the reference, at the end of the paragraph, to Machiavelli, *ibid.,* p. 430. In the Oxford World's Classics edition the two items are on pp. 26 f. and 176.

3. John Speed, *History of Great Britaine* (London, 1611), p. 166.

4. Michael Drayton, *Poly-Olbion,* i.312.

5. Milton, *Comus,* lines 922-23.

6. Pasquale Villari, *Niccolò Machiavelli and his Times,* trans. L. Villari (London, 1878-83), III, 381-82.

7. Sir Walter Ralegh, *History of the World,* I.ii.5 (ed. 1614), p. 31; *Works* (Oxford University Press, 1829), II, 60-61. Matthew Arnold's comments are in his "On the Modern Element in Literature," *Essays in Criticism, Third Series,* ed. E. J. O'Brien (Boston, 1910).

8. On Cardan and Bodin, see *Method for the Easy Comprehension of History By John Bodin, Translated by Beatrice Reynolds* (New York: Columbia University Press, 1945), pp. xix, 232-33.

9. Migne, *Patrologiae . . . Series Latina,* vol. CXCIX (Paris, 1900), col. 852; A. C. Krey, "John of Salisbury's Knowledge of the Classics," *Transactions of the Wisconsin Academy of Sciences, Arts, and Letters,* XVI, Part II (1910), 948-87.

10. Rabelais, Book II, chap. viii.

11. Samuel Eliot Morison, *Three Centuries of Harvard 1636-1936* (Cambridge: Harvard University Press, 1937), pp. 389-90.

12. Joel E. Spingarn, *A History of Literary Criticism in the Renaissance* (New York: Macmillan, 1899 and later editions), p. 3.

CHAPTER II

1. Preface to the *Fables, Essays of John Dryden,* ed. W. P. Ker (Oxford: Clarendon Press, 1900), II, 254 f.; *Poems,* ed. John Sargeaunt (Oxford University Press, 1913), pp. 271-72.

2. *Wilson's Arte of Rhetorique 1560,* ed. G. H. Mair (Oxford: Clarendon Press, 1909), p. 5.

3. Lionel Trilling, *Matthew Arnold* (New York: Norton, 1939), p. 168.

4.   Sir Philip Sidney, "An Apology for Poetry," *Elizabethan Critical Essays,* ed. G. G. Smith (Oxford: Clarendon Press, 1904), I, 178.

5.   George Brandes, *Main Currents in Nineteenth Century Literature* (London: Heinemann; New York: Macmillan, 1906), I, 3.

6.   Spenser's letter to Ralegh, included in editions of *The Faerie Queene.*

7.   *Oeuvres complètes de Ronsard,* ed. H. Vagany (Paris: Garnier, 1923-24), VI, 377.

8.   W. C. Atkinson, "Miguel de Cervantes," *Fortnightly Review* (November, 1947), p. 375.

9.   *Discoveries,* ed. G. B. Harrison (Bodley Head Quartos, 1923), p. 10; *Ben Jonson,* ed. C. H. Herford, Percy and Evelyn Simpson, VIII (Oxford: Clarendon Press, 1947), 567.

10.   *The Faerie Queene,* III.xi.32. Cf. Ovid, *Metam.* vi.109.

11.   Thomas Watson, *Poems,* ed. E. Arber (London, 1870), p. 43.

12.   C. S. Lewis, *The Allegory of Love* (Oxford University Press, 1938), chap. vii.

13.   *The Faerie Queene,* II.xii.61.

14.   *Ibid.,* III.vi.

15.   *Troilus and Cressida,* I.iii.75f.

16.   Franck L. Schoell, *Études sur l'humanisme continental en Angleterre* (Paris: H. Champion, 1926).